WALKI

Steve Ford

WALKING AWAKE

Steve Ford

NON-DUALITY PRESS

For Mandy

———

WALKING AWAKE

First edition published April 2014 by NON-DUALITY PRESS

© Steve Ford 2014
© Non-Duality Press 2014

Steve Ford has asserted his right under the Copyright, Designs
and Patents Act, 1988, to be identified as author
of this work.

Front Cover photograph by *Bread and Shutter*
www.breadandshutter.com

NON-DUALITY PRESS | PO Box 2228 | Salisbury | SP2 2GZ
United Kingdom

ISBN: 978-1-908664-44-0

www.non-dualitypress.org

Contents

DIALOGUES

Foreword

The story of Steve Ford's realisation is unusual. One night in his room in 1999 there was a total falling away of all identification as the personal self. It was unusual in the sense that Steve had no prior experience of spiritual seeking. He had neither teacher nor guru; no paradigm which would explain what had happened. All vestiges of personality were suddenly gone; there was direct and immediate seeing as and from no-thing, from the absolute.

Such accounts exist within the spiritual literature and in each case there appears to follow a period of relative dysfunctionality and subsequent reintegration so that what has happened may be understood and conveyed within the world of form.

In Steve's case this took the form of an exhaustive investigation in consciousness which he eventually came to refer to as The Living Process. He explains that realisation is just the beginning and unless subsequent investigation into the nature of consciousness takes place there is re-identification and consequently self-orientation around no-thing.

Many contemporary teachers and their students relate in this way.

So what follows in this introductory book is the story of Steve's early life, his realisation, enquiry and integration in consciousness, and some interactions that have taken place with some of those who have made their way to be with Steve.

Nathan Gill
Woodlands, September 2013

SEEING FROM BEING

Seeing without thinking. Pure awareness relating from no-thing. Awareness aware of itself. Our true nature is intimacy, love, a love that truly sees with no blemish of self or ego.

But looking into the world of things there is a forgetting to see from no-thing and, in that separation, awareness identifies with things. Awareness identifies with form and what we call ego. It becomes afraid of what it no longer knows (its forgotten formlessness); attention stays fixed in the world of things and begins seeking.

The Living Process came initially from an awakening from full identification with individual self. There was a sudden realisation of awareness relating from the non-personal, or absolute state of being, and from that realisation, awareness no longer needed to construct meaning for itself from the mind, from form. It was purely as *I Am – I Am* being the original thought of *That which Is* – the absolute.

At first the realisation was good enough but after a time there was a coming back into the world looking for more of an understanding of the realisation of truth. I was curious to see how thought and feeling, the outer vehicles of expression, and awareness itself, came into relation to truth.

Old patterned ways of understanding come from experience and experience has come from the world. Awareness in the form of attention has taken the perspective of the outer functionality, of form, rather than its formless knowing that truly sees. Consciousness loses the higher perspective and acquires the shape of form.

In this identification with the unconscious self, awareness then seeks wholeness via the unconscious. Awareness senses its formless nature and tries to peer into the inner true reality. But this is an act of separation which cannot lead to wholeness because it is based on looking at the outer form; it merely leads to further separation. It is only by resting and relating from the formless that one sees into the self and contractions are released. In resting and relating from the formless, from no-thing, the Self in its pseudo-identity as self is no longer seeking wholeness as it knows it *is* wholeness.

So The Living Process was seeing how awareness in realisation moved in recognition of reality while at the same time negotiating form – thought, feeling, relative existence – without becoming identified. I saw how form came into its own imitation of realised consciousness.

I saw that all conditions of consciousness, such as thought and feeling, imitate realised unconditional consciousness in a way that maintains the formless integrity of realisation of true nature. I came to know the formless in form and saw that form is an expression of the formless, and that within every form, is the vast emptiness of being.

Seeing from being is like seeing from the oneness that is in everything, seeing from true nature. You're seeing from a place where there's no memory, feeling or thought. You're seeing from the eternal realm. You see the silence in everything, you see the true nature of things, because, within everything, there is the unmanifest. Even in the most crowded and noisiest place, there's still that silent knowing.

CHILDHOOD

I remember as a child, I would contemplate naturally; by contemplating I mean seeing life happening from the point of view of awareness – awareness which was an unidentified consciousness that related purely from the moment. In this contemplation I watched the flow of life and saw thoughts and feelings as they arose, but – as I later came to recognise – this seeing was unrealised. There was no embodied recognition that would carry such a seeing into the relative world of daily existence.

During one such contemplation I became interested in the mystery of appearance and wondered where it came from. I watched the thought arise: *What if the world had never come into being*? And while I contemplated this thought, I fell into the silence and vastness of no-thing, and my mind disappeared.

As children, we see directly from awareness without the aberration of an identification that captures the attention as we begin to develop ego. This seeing is un-realised – it has not yet come to recognise itself as awareness. Everything is exciting and curious because we see from the mystery and we are curiousness itself. This 'face before you were born' sees without thinking. I spent many hours in this state that is often called daydreaming. It is a stillness that seekers are chasing in the name of awakening – a stillness that sees and moves.

A child sees the information that the senses present, which we call the world, from no-thing. And what people see in the eyes of a child is innocence. Innocence – no-thing – is the prime mover of all things; it is the flow of consciousness that comes from no-thing, giving meaning to 'all things that arise' out of no-thing. This innocence of a child's seeing becomes lost when ego is acquired, as a defence against all that is perceived as 'other', in the journey through the years to adulthood.

Hence the saying that we should 'become as little children'.

Contemplation was the space to be for me as a child, and my body, too, would go into its own stillness. I could escape what I thought of as the world while seeing from/as awareness. There was conflict in the world: Dad drank heavily and Mum would fight it. There were nights of pots-and-pans mayhem as I was frozen with fear, listening and feeling the violent reverberations of disagreement between the two adults. I learned very young that you cannot reason with alcohol and so I escaped often into the stillness that was available to me.

Despite always being able to see from no-thing the outer parts of me began to imitate the world and its conditioning norms and values. And so my seeing remained unrealised, as it does with most of us in our presumed identity as egoically based individuals. Awareness arises as attention and becomes 'caught' within the limitations of thought and identity.

A SHOCK

At eighteen I learned that the man whom I'd known all my life as 'Father' was not in fact my biological father. I was devastated. I felt stupid and betrayed because all of my life I'd looked at him and wanted one day to be like him; as his presumed first-born I felt I had that right. No longer was this the case. The role now fell to my younger brother who was in fact his biological son.

Where there had been the want there was now a *Why?* Also, there was the question: *Who am I?* My identity had been pulled from under my feet in an instant and the most important thing was that question: *Who am I?*

It's difficult to know what it's like to find out you're an illegitimate son, unless you have experienced it directly. Its effect on identity can be traumatic, and it can also answer many questions all too quickly. Straightaway I resolved to not be like anyone else ever again, and I went away to find out who I was. The family in which I grew up failed in providing me with that reality. I couldn't hang around – too much had happened. I was angry and needed answers, and the family didn't have them. I was given my birth certificate with my real name – Stephen Ford – different to the name I had always answered to. I didn't know who this person was.

DRINK AND RECOVERY

Alcohol came my way – I felt I needed it. It drowned the feelings that raged within. I would drink into blackout, and soon I drank compulsively – that is to say I drank alcoholically. I drank alcoholically for ten years, and it was during this time that I became increasingly unaware of who I was. There was much experimenting with playing the roles of artist and poet, but I was neither. I was pretentious and delusional. I was unhappy and angry, but too confused to see it. My drink days were dark days that took me further into separation – separation being the inability to express and know myself from my true nature. I played with appearance, using thought and the perceptual framework in an egoic way.

The mid-eighties to mid-nineties were just a blur. I tried so many times to better myself, including going to college and studying art. Drink always got in the way and bit by bit, my ambition decreased to a point where one day I woke up and knew within my heart that I was a drunk, and all I really wanted to do was drink. It was an epiphany. I was very accepting of this fact and my self-worth was nil. All the arrests for drunk and disorderly, the outbursts of anti-social madness – it was all I really knew.

My drinking days came to an end when I was back home living with my mother. It wasn't a good idea, so it was while I was there that I resolved to deal with the drink problem. I confided in a friend about this. His response was to give me a room at his place so that I could be away from the pressures of living with family. The condition was that I agree to go to a 12 Step self-help group as part of stopping drinking. I agreed – it seemed the reasonable thing.

I went to my first 12 Step meeting in January 1995 and I got sober in October 1995. I kept attending meetings even when I kept relapsing. Relapsing would always give way to a part of me that needed to be challenged as part of my ongoing commitment to recovery. Any reservation had to go.

While attending the 12 Step fellowship meetings I did as suggested and 'worked the programme' – a programme which is designed for living and going beyond addiction. The 12 Steps are spiritual and practical principles that can be applied to a person's life to help negotiate negative mental and emotional self-destructive patterns, and then to integrate higher discernment and a value system.

I was told from the beginning to be rigorously honest, but I couldn't. I couldn't find my voice. Instead, I related purely from the mechanics and process of the Steps. After about two years of this relating and using the Steps I was found to be good at doing so. After three years of practising this way of life, instead of living with active addiction, my life had been enhanced beyond my wildest dreams. I could share my recovery with others – but it only consisted of a word-play that came from a prescribed way of understanding.

After three years I was feeling good, but the ideal began to break. There was something deeper than thought and feeling that wanted to express itself and I hadn't a way to relate to/from it. I'd come to the limitations of my will and my perceptual field of reality. Now I was frightened. Up until now the programme had worked but something else inside of me was dying, something that the programme could only point at, something that only I alone could *be*. But I felt alienated – I still didn't know who I was. And then, something quite remarkable happened.

WHAT THE TUTOR SAID

At that time I was at college so that I could go on to study theology and philosophy at university. I was enrolled in an access course in humanities, designed to bring mature students to entry level of university, and part of my course was studying sociology.

The remarkable thing happened one day while attending a sociology class. I was always the most intense of debaters in the class. Often people would rather I took notes than have an intense debate. I was intense, I didn't know reality and I wanted to know.

That day, at the end of the class, I was still debating when everyone had left the room. Only the tutor and I remained. I can't remember what it was I was debating, all I remember is the tutor raising her hand as I was in mid-flow of argument. She said, 'You're not your thoughts or your feelings.' I stopped very abruptly and became silent; no one had ever told me that before. I was left speechless, and, I was left knowing also that what she said was true – it resonated.

DISINTEGRATION

The next few weeks and months saw me disintegrate. The tutor's words stayed with me. My carefully constructed understanding of recovery began to break down. When I was sharing I would suddenly stop. I felt huge self-obsession. I felt dishonest. I was back in the dis-ease. I was coming out of denial, but coming into a realm of unknowing. I had to go into unknowing, for what I knew was breaking down; all my defences had broken down. They simply did not work anymore.

I stopped going to 12 Step meetings. I couldn't function and was falling apart, and using the programme in the way to which I had become accustomed seemed too dishonest. Staying away from meetings felt instinctually right. At that same time, I stopped attending college for I couldn't function there either. I was left with a deep knowing that something was wrong. I was falling apart, but there was nothing I could do.

DEATH OF SELF AND AWAKENING

Now that I had let go of the 12 Steps and college, I found myself alone in my apartment one evening. In a sudden moment, I found myself kneeling in the middle of the living room floor, knowing that I'd come to the end of *me*. I knew that if something didn't change I was sure to drink again, and I knew with certainty that to drink would be to die. The intuition arose that I had to give up everything. I remembered what the tutor had said – that I am not my thoughts and feelings – and I knew I had come to the point where I had to really let go. I had no idea what lay beyond the giving up of all that I knew, but there is a deep knowing when something is right, even when you do not have the thoughts and feelings to guide you.

I knelt before what I felt to be the unknown. I felt ready to hand over my will. I knew that what I had called 'will' up until that point consisted of my thoughts and feelings and the way that I was manipulating them. First, I gave back my thinking, and as I did I felt loss, a sadness. Sadness that I had been given the capacity to think but now I had to hand it back. There was a sense of failure, but stronger than that was the certainty that I must remain true to surrender of the thinking capacity. I consented to this surrendering and in that moment I felt my thoughts fly away like a flock of birds as the stream of consciousness became non-identified. Suddenly there was no thinking, just a present spaciousness where there had been mental activity. Now, there was just a peace that I'd never known before. I was letting go of my imaginings and was no longer identified with thought as a main principle of my reality. I'd now come to know mind without being identified with it, and within it there was just a presence.

No longer identified with the mental outer body, I began to fall deeper into awareness, a deeper reality of knowing – a knowing without thinking. As my thinking went and my mind opened I was aware of just being aware – empty awareness. As awareness, I was no longer caught within the mental identified structure, no longer was I the same as 'my' thought. There was then a falling below the level where thought resides, as awareness becoming aware of itself is formless and not thought-bound. It was clear that thought is only an outer crystallised and conditioned consciousness and it is as awareness that one falls below into a deeper reality. Attachment to any condition maintains only a state of identification, or 'I'.

As awareness fell deeper, there was a sudden pull to my heart and I felt pain there as the heart's contraction began to relax. There was no longer an egoic contraction holding it in the shape of a conditioned reality, and instead it began to simply open. The opening of my heart was going beyond the deepest contraction. The heart's emotionally conditioned contraction was all that I knew as emotion – the deepest aspect of attachment – deeper patterns than those of the mental plane, conditioned responses that signalled attraction or aversion. Now, without the ego's outer pull from the mind I was falling into my heart. The deeper I went the more open my heart was becoming… and there was pain.

The awareness of pain without ego identification made for clean pain, not the pain of suffering. I could see for the first time that suffering is a resistance to reality. It was in the undoing, in the heart-opening, that I came to know the true loss and pain of what suffering concealed – the pain of separation. A voice in my head said: *This is what you have been running away from all of your life*. I could see that I had never lived beyond the contraction, I had never been free to express, but now, I went into the pain, going beyond anything I had ever known. I was seized with the most profound terror and fear of death.

As the heart opened there was a whooshing sound, a vortex feeling of being pulled into the heart; the pull was not accompanied by mind. As pure awareness, I was returning *home*. I was afraid but I had to consent. I couldn't use any will or protection. I was surrendering, I was going into the void. I consented and I went deep into the heart, a dark deep beyond all knowing, beyond mind. I consented, and then 'I' as ego – a presumed separate entity based on identified thought and emotion – died. At the point of death there was nothing; and then there was a coming to. I could see.

I awoke and could see from formless awareness. There was a complete and stunning stillness. There was just where I saw from, and a seeing into. There was nothing else – no 'me' as ego, only consciousness, a consciousness that was conscious of itself. I could see from the unmanifest. I was in being and being was in me – there was no distinction. There was a complete merging of absolute reality and its expression of clean consciousness. The thought arose: *No one could have shown me this.* I was in awe.

It was late in the evening when I experienced the return to formless awareness, the going beyond everything I'd ever known. Soon after that I went to bed. As I lay in bed I wondered if I'd wake up in the morning and still be the liberated consciousness that could see and relate from the absolute – I wasn't sure. Only when I awoke the following morning did I realise that the liberation was still a way of being – I was still realised.

Life was good – how could it not be? Up until then the world was perceived by my senses, and as consciousness I identified with my outer perceptions of things. Now, though, I could directly relate from no-thing – the formlessness that gave meaning to everything beyond any understanding. I could see the true nature of all things because I could see from the same beingness that was in all things. As consciousness exploring and not identifying, I saw the emptiness that underlay everything. Living from this standpoint was easy as I was *That which Is*, which is in everything without relative location. It was all one.

A NEW WAY OF LIFE

From the standpoint of the fellowship and the 12 Steps, I knew with certainty that I had had an awakening. The true freedom was its own evidence, not that there was a need for anyone to explain, or confirm it. Truth is truth, there is no negotiation – you know. After a few days I went back to a meeting where I saw a friend. She was 'in recovery' and I'd known her since I'd first got into recovery myself. I went up to her and said, 'Hi, I'm ok now, I'm real.' For the first time in my life, I knew I was real – I just wanted to connect. She looked at me and I could tell just from that look that she did not understand what I'd said. I was quite amazed. Having had a spiritual awakening, I thought I'd also recognise others who had awakened but I soon learned that it wasn't like that.

The first few days of awakening were like entering into a whole new dimension – a dimension that just *was*, which no thinking could capture, nor give any true meaning to. It was enough to just *be*. I could see direct from the eternal, from formlessness. There was no longer any image coming between what I first was as *being*, and the world. It was as if truth was seeing through my eyes, and yet I and the *one* were the same. It was a state of true humility and there was a not wanting to do anything with it. The self had changed in its orientation. Now there was a relating from the absolute, and the expression of that was the pure knowing of that.

As consciousness, there had been an awakening – a recognition of the origin of consciousness, namely *That* which Is being. Only then could consciousness see its true function, namely that of knowing true nature. Only then was there a realignment to reality: before that, consciousness was caught in form, identified, not knowing its origin, understanding only an image that had been carved and created out of the imagery of a life's experience. This identification had been the illusion that had separated my true understanding of reality, but with realisation, I could see that experience is only form and memory; the expression of memory is thought. Now, though, there was a differentiating between clean consciousness and thought. Thought was an image whereas consciousness remained formless.

It was ambiguous to the mind. I could sense the likeness of truth running through myself as a capacity to express truth. The recognition of truth was all-pervasive, in itself it was the expression. The recognition came in a few ways. I sensed an eternal likeness, and realised that eternity was *now*, and always has been, and that there had never been time. Time had purely been an outer expression, a creation of the mind. Time existed only in a dimension that was relative, like all other aspects of the functioning self. Seeing from the eternal was seeing from the now; the self, in its relative function, could only reflect that. Everything that is expressed by the five senses first has its origin in the eternal expression of the absolute. Instead of the ambiguous understanding based on the five senses, there had been a total shift of consciousness leading to a total change in perspective. Instead of relating from the outer looking for truth, there was instead a seeing directly from reality into the conditioned meaning of outer contracted expression, which was ultimately a reflection of that intimate reality.

I was free and awake, and in the world. The world became new. Seeing from the eternal absolute,

I could see that reality in everything without the 'I' stealing it. Ego identification was seen as a distortion whereby consciousness compromises its formless identity to relate from mind form, but mind form is only memory. This way of relating steals from you the direct experience of all things and instead gives you only the memory of things as a basis to relate and experience. Instead of perceiving things from a perceptual framework, I was seeing into the nature of all things and seeing from the nature of all things. True nature is the underlying reality of all; it is oneness. It was amazing to see creation and all things relating from the one, in the absence of the I. There was now the direct experience of all things, relating from the non-located oneness. I walked out into the streets of where I lived continuing to be free. The town centre was alive beneath the banal veneer of industrial design. I was free, liberated.

It was amazing to see people all 'not here'. The *here* was eternal and was not mind, but I could see people caught within the self-protecting mental projections that we call 'ego'. I was stunned to see that I was not of the world (the outer projection of reality) anymore, for where I was relating from was being denied by their minds. My mind perceived truth only to reflect and allow it through so that thought was recognition, and not a projection.

It seemed only natural. I walked as if invisible. Without self-concept there was just an invisible pure awareness that I had no choice to be. To see *me* was to see nothing, self-obsession had dissipated.

The absolute non-personal awareness was all-pervading, within and without everything. Life became increasingly simple. The complexity of self-obsession had fallen away to leave only a non-personal awareness that could not be characterised – rather, it could only be reflected.

I was a different person. I had left college, and had come away from my friends in recovery. It was the spring of 1999. I knew I could get a summer season working on the old steam passenger boats on the Thames. The Thames, as Sir Winston Churchill once said, is 'the silver thread that runs through England'. I spent the summer crewing. It was easy work, and the Thames was an ideal place to just *be*.

That summer of '99 was good. I knew I had awakened, there was no negotiation, I was free. I wanted to see other awakened people and I began looking. It was pure curiosity, a wanting to connect with someone else, with others, from the standpoint of *That* from which I was seeing. So I began talking to people. I had a limited catalogue of words that could describe and express truth but it was enough to get by. I had close friends who, like me, were recovered from addiction of some sort, whether they were primary addictions (those of drink and drugs) or process addictions (those of co-dependency, gambling, sex and love).

I knew my friends were working towards awakening, and that people have their own experience of spirituality. From them I'd hear the thoughts and feelings on spirituality but never did I see the absolute silent penetrating glance you would get from absolute reality. What had happened in my case was the awakened state that preceded perception and preceded thought. It was, is, and shall ever be *That which Is*, and I was of *That*, as an empty awareness no longer identified with outer forms of expression.

I was careful, though, not to describe the awakening to others just at the drop of a hat. I knew what it had taken for me to let go of the perceived meaning of everything that I had ever known to be true – it was a terrifying overwhelming happening. I began instead to be discreet, and gentle, due largely to a conversation I had with a Buddhist I met while on a training day working as an outreach drugs worker. I had to go into London and work for a day at a prescribing unit that also functioned as a drop-in centre for drug and alcohol related issues.

There was a girl who worked there. She was roughly the same age as me and looked very spiritual, wearing her Buddhism outside of herself – beads and other symbols. I had known of Buddhism before the awakening and had seen how it had attracted a lot of young people, intellectual people. I thought if I asked her about truth, I might learn whether or not she was realised. I asked her with her permission whether she thought she was her thoughts and feelings. I remember to this day the look on her face – she looked perplexed and slightly horrified.

I became more careful in my questioning. I wanted to know. I was curious. I wanted to connect with someone who had the same knowing. Just as thought connects with thinking, being connects with being without using thought. If unrealised, thought will distort being – there is instead a projection rather than realised reflection. I was looking for clean connections, not that I was aware in any discursive way – it was more a knowing.

The desire to find others who had had an experience that was similar to mine just fell away after a while. Instead, I began to just get on with life. I had a few friends with whom I would talk about this rare awareness that can relate from truth. They saw me as true to what I was talking about. The draw to me was by life experience. They had had similar backgrounds and were in the fellowship. With a recovery angle, and a psychological interpretation, I would talk about what was real and what was not.

By this time I was a father to a new-born baby, and fresh out of college. I had no idea of what I wanted to do regarding career. It seemed all ambition had left me. The only thing that mattered was the reality that I had come to know. The new perspective and the view from it was all that really meant anything. Everything else was secondary. But I had to do something as I was living in the world with the responsibilities of parenthood.

OUTREACH & COUNSELLING

I saw a job advertised for a drugs outreach worker and I knew that if I did that work it would lead to other possibilities. I got the job, which entailed setting up the outreach service by myself. It was a new service run by local councils, initiated by the government's plan to have more addicted people in treatment. My job was to meet the addicted population while out and about walking the streets and visiting hospitals and institutions. I spent two years working in outreach until it came to an end in 2001. In those early years of the programme I was able, without too much pressure, to earn a living, and not be confined to a heavy structure that demanded me to come away from the reality that I was exploring in terms of awakening. There was freedom to explore, and explore I did. The work was part-time, so there was a lot of free time to just *be*.

I've always found people interesting. Ever since being a child I would listen more than talk, not out of obedience, but out of pure curiosity. I loved people's stories, and now I was amongst the most fascinating – sometimes sad – stories of people on the streets or in hospital and other institutions.

I spent those two years wandering around and doing my job, just seeing from no-thing. I kept one eye open in case there was someone else awakened in the same way that I was, but there was not. I don't wish to sound arrogant; it just confirmed – before I fully realised it – how rare this awareness of the absolute was in people's lives. I'd awakened; my deepest knowing of truth reflected that. I was humble in knowing that it had nothing to do with *me*. For that very reason it kept me grounded. I hadn't done anything, but we live in a world obsessed with doing. It seemed everyone was doing and, in that, they were missing the vital clue to who they really are.

During the time spent working in outreach, I was never ambitious. I was happy to just *be* and to carry on with the work required of me. I was involved in reality – just being and reflecting; that was enough. No job satisfaction could offer nearly enough compared to conscious liberation. I would often see people who were ambitious and I simply did not connect with that. I usually connected more with people who had nothing much in terms of worldly interest. I liked just being with people who didn't have compulsive drives that took them away from the gentle way of being that gave true meaning to existence. Work could never compensate for that love, and true meaning.

Other life commitments were calling at this time. My first daughter was growing up and I had to support my family, so it was time to get a job that was more substantial than the part-time outreach work that I'd been doing. It was with gratitude that I left that job as it had shown me a lot and fed my curiosity, allowing me to move. More importantly, those two years of walking in the city were a time of reflection and integration which gave me the idea for the title *Walking Awake*.

I found a post as a trainee counsellor in 2001 with a charity that worked in the field of addiction in prisons. Before this I had no intention of becoming a counsellor. At the time, the image I had of counsellors was very poor. My perception of a therapist was a person who just nodded their head at you while listening and saying, 'So how does that make you feel'. A cliché, but that was my perception and, as a result, I had no interest in counselling or counsellors. For some reason, though, working for a charity as a counsellor in prisons and using the 12 Steps appealed to my curiosity. I had nothing to lose, I would gain full training at least.

I was working with young offenders who were not too much younger than I was, and I began to gain an understanding of how counsellors worked with people in addiction – addiction being a denial mechanism against intimacy and reality. It proved to be fascinating to see how the counsellors worked, for all the ones that I worked with had different approaches. I learned a lot.

MEETING WITH PEOPLE

In 2006 I went to a 12 Step meeting. Michael, an old friend, and I were the only two to turn up. We hadn't seen each other for a few years so it was good to meet again. Michael told me about about meetings that he had been attending exploring reality. I'd never heard of this kind of meeting before. He said that there are certain teachers that sit quietly and, after a while, people ask them questions, and he then quoted something he had heard one of the speakers had said. I can't remember what the quote was but I do remember smiling and saying, 'Yes, that is true'. Michael looked at me sharply and said, 'You understand that?' To which I replied, 'Yes, I said it's true'. Michael commented that not many people would understand that. He then asked, "If you were to ask a teacher a question, what would you ask?" *Good question*. I thought. After a moment I said, "I would ask, 'Is truth just is, as is?'" Michael looked surprised. He said that his teacher called reality 'as is'. I agreed. Michael then said, "I have a friend I would like you to meet. His name is David

The next week Michael introduced me to David. We met and talked many times. One day, David asked me why I didn't look at his eyes when communicating. I didn't know why, was the honest answer. I'd become introverted with my internal reality, not able to share that with anyone. I'd come away from the world but didn't reflect this from my own recognition of being. I looked, and stared at David. I looked him in the eyes. There was an instant connection. The room disappeared; the flow of concentration was a pure energy that had been released like water from a dam. David asked, 'Do you realise that not everyone would be comfortable with this gaze?' He then went on to say that he loved it, and the flow of energy was good. We maintained eye contact for the next hour or so.

My interaction with David at this time was important. He was the first person to have mirrored my seeing; I was beginning to understand the effects of seeing without thinking. We spent many hours together talking about the nature of reality. I would share my seeing, and he would place it in the context of how a seeker would understand what I was saying. He knew that seekers would be interested in what I could share, and where I could see from.

From then on, I began meeting other people, seekers from Bristol and London. We began to sit around at David's house and enquire into the nature of reality. People would ask questions from a mind perspective, but they would often be disappointed or frustrated when, in a deep state of contemplation, I would answer in a way that could not be understood by the thinking mind. Seeing is always and only understood by a knowing that is deeper than outer forms of thought, feeling, intuition and will. Reality cannot be understood; it can only be lived. Thought cannot merge with, or absorb what you first are. Thought can only connect with thought, and thought is form. What we first are, is formless, and what is formless is consciousness which has no identification with anything.

When consciousness becomes identified with something, it loses its formless integrity. Knowing becomes identified with the appearance of self and, for most people, their mind reflects this fixated way of perceiving. I was humbled to see this via the empty recognition of pure awareness.

I began to embody a deeper understanding and integration from those early meetings where we would sit and contemplate. I would let go of everything and relate purely from being. From the deepest mystery a seeing without thinking would come – so deep the room would fill with light and all definition and sense of individuality would disappear.

EXPLORING

I was beginning to undcrstand the awakening in a living way. This means that, as I was seeing from a knowing, the mind was reflecting that in my attention of being, an attention that I recognsed as *I am*. Mind naturally reflects your current state of consciousnes. In a state of separation, the mind will reflect the distortion of identification with the outer reflecting bodies of existence, thus creating a 'me', an 'I'. When consciousness is relating from being, the mind reflects no-thing as the primary reality instead of reflecting the 'I'.

I knew that relating direct from being was not for everyone. Some people would rather not speak or hear anything; they would rather feel the presence, and for them it was just about truth, without any interpretation. There were others also who seemed to come from the other way. These people would go forward in their enquiry intellectually until their thought was met with resonance of truth. There would then be a coming together for them in truth.

I found the process interesting. I hadn't been a seeker in the way that I came to know seekers in the sense of non-duality. I had simply been looking to get honest, as the dishonesty of my previous living had been killing me. I now recognised that the honesty I was looking for was reality. I'd never known reality in the relative sense, I'd only ever had a knowing that was unrealised in the self, deep down in a place I'd cut off from as a child. In becoming honest, I'd become real. I'd fallen into a realised consciousness that could now relate by pure, intimate knowing. This was the same knowing that the seekers were asking about but they wanted awakening in the sense of enlightenment or truth – not the honesty that I had been seeking.

I came from no school of spiritual or philosophic exploration, I knew only the 12 Steps, which were devised as a programme of recovery that had worked for me. I'd stopped drinking, and the Steps then enabled me to remain stopped. Working the principles in my daily life, my life became more functional. The last step speaks of having had an awakening, and I did have an awakening. The awakening aspect of the programme is not pointing at any one description of true reality, rather it alludes to living a spiritual life where the new recourse for life comes from within.

Awakening seemed to be an uncommon awareness, a consciousness that was conscious of its
origin, an origin that just *is*, with no location and,
of course, the fellowship didn't come forward in
great numbers to say that I'd finally got it, even
though that's what I expected at first.

Now, though, I was sitting with people who knew
of this awareness. Their questions were direct. As I
spoke, I explored, and as I explored, I was beginning to embody. For some years there had been no
questions. I had simply enjoyed the pure awareness,
without expressing it outwardly. This dynamic had
begun to become painful, though. The inner world
of the absolute can be seen while at the same time
not being expressed in the outer conventional way of
living; but in not expressing it, there is compromise.
I recognised that this was what had happened with
me to some degree, but now that I was speaking in
response to other people's questions, their enquries
were pulling me into a superficial way of being that
was just beginning to reflect a deeper, more absolute
and permanent reality. Not only could I see from
and as the absolute, now I was beginning to express
my seeing – they were becoming one.

Around this time I was invited to speak on
Conscious TV. I was interviewed specifically about
the realisation that had occurred in 1999 and chose
not to speak about what was now happening. It

was obvious to me that full integration had not yet taken place.

MEETING HANNAH

Meetings continued to be my playground of integration. But that playground was to extend beyond the meetings when I met Hannah. David had spoken of me to Hannah and had arranged a meeting for us. I connected with her straightaway – with Hannah, I could merge in a way where we both lived the same recognition.

We would meet on a Tuesday and go for long walks until one day my heart responded. I told Hannah about this, but she already knew. We stood up and walked away.

I hadn't been looking for this sort of relationship, as my previous long-term relationship had come to an end not long before meeting Hannah. I'd had no time to be alone in order to establish where I was as an individual appearing in the world, with unresolved issues that remained to be resolved in the light of conscious awakened living. We'd come together when I was talking with people about the nature of reality and only just beginning to embody it.

We would sit for many hours connecting and merging in being. What was beneficial at the beginning of our relationship was that it allowed me to begin to explore these deeper parts of my humanity and the hidden patterns that remained unintegrated. I still had unresolved emotional questions from having come from a previous long term relationship, and whereas my connection with Hannah was beautiful while seeing from the depths of formless awareness, the remaining dysfunctional areas in my life – by which I mean the life of Steve the person – would at times divide and separate that inner connection through the conflict of outer personality traits.

Hannah and I knew that in the end it was clear that I needed time and that the relationship should finish. We were both sad even though we had both sensed it coming. We were both still connected but the dysfunction at the level of personality simply did not serve the inner life.

GOING IT ALONE

It seemed that there was only one other place to go. I had to go *home* again, back to no-thing, and learn to come through into the relative life of functional being and relating on my own. Without Hannah, though, I felt so alone. Where so far I'd shared the journey, nothing seemed to touch me any more in the same way, and it was to be like that for some time. It was now that I learned the biggest truth of all: how to integrate – how to move from, and as, formless awareness into full embodied functioning as a person in the world. I came to know it as The Living Process.

In earlier meetings with groups of people, I had tended to talk from formless awareness in a way that they didn't really understand. I realised that I now had to learn to move in the world and to be able to speak with people about the awakening and how it related but in a language I was yet to develop. It always felt that in awareness I was in the absolute and the absolute was in me, but now, more than ever, I knew I had to bring that awareness fully through into functional life. I must be able to be in anything, any form, while still remaining as *Who I Am* without compromising that formless identity.

At that time, I was working for the criminal justice system, delivering drug and alcohol programmes to offenders. For six months the work I did there was the only structure in my life. Every other aspect of my life came under review. The pressing question that arose was: *How do I move from That which Is? How does the essence of what I am come into the creation in a living way?* I was curious to know. I began to be with the question in an intuitive way where I would relax and hold the intention.

There was no real timeline to this process. Life became an acceptance once again of anything and everything. It didn't matter what I felt, or what thoughts came into mind, it was all to be seen – and to be seen until I knew how to move. My life situation became the Buddha's Bodhi Tree, and I was to accept it until I had the full realisation of what the true movement was, and how it related from innermost being, to the outermost form and expression.

I can't remember how long I was just being with whatever was happening in the self. When I say 'self' I use the word to describe the capacity, in a human way, to express and reflect a way of being. The self is our capacity to think thoughts, feel feelings, a sense of physicality, sensuality. In one sense it is form, a form that has inner being that is formless. With awakening, though, there is a relating from the formless being, allowing the outer form (self) to reflect that when integrated. Unawakened, there is not the reflecting of what you first are as being; rather, there is identifying with thought, and it is in this identification that consciousness is divided by the self rather than reflected. When consciousness identifies with thought – thought divided in a dualistic way – you become an 'I' with likes, and dislikes, without the knowing of the deeper unified reality.

FULL REINTEGRATION

One morning I got off the train to go to work. I stood as awareness, purely aware of everything.

I was aware of the external form, and the internal reaction of inner forms – thoughts, feelings and physical sensations. As consciousness, as pure awareness, I was accepting everything inner and outer. My question had been: *What is the true movement*? In the anticipation of an answer, I remained simply aware. Being aware was all I knew to do, the only action left. I knew that doing anything with a mind orientation would negate any knowing. I was to stay in my knowing. I knew this meant the letting go of everything. I knew about seeing from no-thing, but I didn't know how to move from it. This seemed the only certain knowing, everything else was just a happening.

Having let go, I had no care anymore for any outer security to distract me. All natural-born instincts were on hold. Financial insecurity had no hold anymore, not that it had had a big hold anyway, but it certainly pulls hard. There was a relief to be standing purely in knowing. I understood now the meaning of poverty being a naked awareness knowing its true need for realisation, like Christ and his need to know god. I knew the Christ awareness was the empty unattached knowing of true absolute reality.

I would go through the working days aware of my functional role, and allowing the whole day to be a meditation that I allowed as awareness to experience while maintaining formless knowing. One particular day a probation worker was discussing an issue about a client with me. I could see her within her role of 'offender management' going through her professionally trained discernment 'regarding client issues'. I knew it was all on a mental level. I stayed in my knowing, allowing only the understanding of what was going on to be a function that I as awareness was experiencing. Staying in relation to the formless reality that I had come to know as 'the deep' had a profound effect on the immediate life situation. I began to fall deeper into the deep, and as there was a deeper being, the offender manager stopped talking – her mind stopped. She looked confused, saying that she had lost her thinking. This was disorientating for her as she was still in relation to her thinking rather than the deeper reality of this moment.

I was coming away from the world of identification again. Letting go of the patterning and being just aware. During the occasional contact I had with people, I rested as awareness in their company. I felt dysfunctional as, at that point, I hadn't learned to relate from the knowing. At that time, I could not see the link between the knowing of reality, and the conditioned response to it. I continued to wait as awareness. I would often sense a non-coordination between what I knew as liberated being, and what arose within the perceptual field of awareness. Personality traits and thoughts arose as a conditioned, personal response, but it was unconscious, it was not rooted in the living essence of what I first knew to be true. I was just continuing to be aware. Being totally empty was to be unidentified with all happening, just remaining aware. I got used to it. In the beginning, there was an awkwardness in remaining in knowing and being with people. There were social, collective versions of *I* and *me* that people expected to see. I got used to being the non-reactive knowing.

Looking back at that first awakening as formless awareness, I saw how difficult this early stage of awakening can be, for it is just the beginning. I had awoken within the confines of a conventional life, far removed from a setting like a monastery or ashram, where there is traditional guidance on such awakening. Rather, I had been living a life with a partner and a young daughter, and other priorities. It also coincided with a new career. I was 31 years old. Conventional living seemed to be a set-up running on automated lines. Time structure, hierarchy and social conventions – all patterned automatically. There appeared to be conditioning upon conditioning within conventional paradigms, layers of psychological conditioning.

I could see through the conditioning to the core

of being in everything. I could see people's identifications as a kind of sleeping; but behind the confines of that sleeping there was reality, in everyone. It simply remained unrealised. It seemed I knew more in that initial awakening, but within the next seven years I had become dulled into submission to a reality of not knowing how to move, how to express. *How do I relate from truth in all of my affairs?* This question haunted me. Just as before awakening the movement of seeking is relentless and unstoppable, now, the growing in the likeness of truth was unstoppable. It appeared that, whether realised or unrealised in truth, we are relentlessly pulled to truth.

As I persisted in my waiting enquiry, I began to notice that instead of being confined to the fine awareness of truth my awareness was now becoming broader in the experience of truth. I was allowing awareness to go anywhere where there was a pull to go, and it became ever more clear to me that awakening wasn't just about becoming still and going deeply in to see out. My outer form, emotional and mental, began falling in on me bit by bit. The identity structures that did not relate from a realised knowing would pull from my consciousness. I would just see, and in the seeing fall through each patterned illusion to find a deeper memory that was the origin of the abstract illusion that contracted in the body. Going into the memory was all that was needed for it to open and breathe and be released. Contraction is a holding, an area in the consciousness of the apparent individual that appears to be frozen into a kind of tightness that forgets to breathe and live. Contractions, when seen, begin to imitate consciousness by opening. Realised attention itself was fast becoming the therapist, the physician.

Life was becoming more like it was when I first awakened. There was that same sense of a renewal, a new liberation. I could move as a realised I, *I Am*, I could be anywhere. Most importantly, I could now merge with patterns that arose out of the self, namely conditioning. Instead of being awareness fixated with being, I became a knower of truth, the realisation of truth that could move through the self. This I began to see as a growing maturity. An attention remaining upon *That which Is* is the very movement of *That which Is*. Form appeared now to be nothing more than an ongoing condition that imitated the experiencer – experiencer as realised. The realised experiencer was nothing more than realised consciousness in its merging with form without losing formless integrity – recognition.

In the 1999 awakening, becoming formless, I was aware of truth, but not who I was in relation to truth. Now, I was becoming realised, not just awakened. I could be formless in everything, maintaining the suchness (the direct experience) of all experience without there being anyone there. Being in the world of sense perception, but not of it. Merging with all things, relating from the nature of all things, I saw that merging is a meeting with appearances while maintaining a conscious formless identity of presence. The ego identifies with form, thus everything is usually interpreted by mind definition, thought and emotional precedence. With formless conscious awareness, there is no definition, only direct experience as formlessness, a formlessness now in relation to the ground of all being.

I was no longer stuck. I was exploring as unidentified curiousness, an emptiness, a knowing that merged with everything. Everything in my life came under review again. Internally I was now aware of thought and feeling and experiencing them from formlessness: letting them in without restriction. Letting everything into no-thing and going into everything as no-thing. I began to see a living process appear. A wonderful transmutation without anyone doing anything, conceptual or intentional. I saw that there was a correlation between form and the formless. The more I became formless, the deeper I went into form, and the deeper it came into being. For the first time I was seeing how form that comprised the mental and emotional layerings of outer consciousness responded directly to a consciousness that was conscious of itself.

Before realisation of the formless consciousness being the realised I, the awareness could only reflect a way of being as a recognition and not a movement. For being to become a movement means that, as awareness, attention becomes totally empty, unidentified with outer appearance. This state of unidentified awareness allows for an opening that administers an essence of pure being. Through emptiness, attention becomes a streaming of realisation, commonly known as transmission; one's realised attention carries the very essence of absolute. This transmission is the realised attention that relates from source, from non-located absolute.

As a formless awareness we merge as a true movement of being. It is then that it's seen that all things arise out of the one. Everything has its origin in the absolute, the one. Our awareness then becomes the movement of that essence, a creative dynamic of everything appearing without there being a separate self. I could understand now why I did not know this upon awakening. Awakening was the beginning. Now I was growing and maturing in the likeness of that truth, as awareness aware of itself, without identification apart from *That which Is true*, a knowing that proved to be a formless identity. This knowing began to experience in the likeness of my true nature; form was just a mirror of the deepest of experience, deeper than the perceptual field.

This was the fact of being formless: that form appeared, and was experienced; but now, the experience was the formless consciousness and there was no division. Division only existed when form was identified with as a discrete identity, as a contracted sense of being an individual. Now, the individual sense of *Steve* would arise out of the formless awareness that identified its origin with being and maintaining expression of that being.

FLOW OF ATTENTION

Experiencing life as formless awareness, I was being what I am in truth. True identity was in awareness in its knowing of being, knowing of a deeper reality than form for its own definition, and expression. I was in the world of sense perception and identification – but not of it. Confusion about what the true movement was dissipated, for I now knew the merging factor between unmanifest and manifest. As knowing, I was a flow of attention that remained unattached, unidentified from any outer reflection of form for definition.

Looking back, I could see that waiting with the intent of knowing was what revealed this awareness – there was no thinking about it. As soon as there was realisation, I could see this understanding in teachers and holy books. The awareness itself is *I Am*. It is that which Nisargadatta Maharaj spoke of as *I Am That*. The *I Am* is the realised awareness knowing of its unmanifest origin and function. The unmanifest origin is *That*, simply *That*. *I Am That*. This means that *Am* is a conscious reflection of *That* which cannot be defined by any means of mind, it simply *is*. It can only be known by awareness without identification with form.

I was simply being and knowing while the world continued its course. I was curious. I was observing everyone again, as I did in the beginning when I awoke to true nature. I began to go deeper into the no-thing – into the absolute no-thing.

WALKING AWAKE

One Sunday morning I found myself walking through Chinatown in London, after seeing a client at my Soho office. I saw people milling about but I was not engaged in thinking about what was going on. I was just walking when suddenly I dropped into a deeper state of consciousness. People were just happening in the formless reality that was everywhere. The very appearance of the street and the people was so transient that the only reality was reality itself – the permanent *That which Is*. Now, instead of the expression being confined to a satsang in a room of stilled respect, it was in living movement and observation from itself into itself, while appearance danced upon that empty reality that was the promise of all existence.

Standing now in knowing was all I wanted. I was no one but everything, without judgement or use of self. I let everything fall away again so as to just simply know and be.

I had awakened again, this time into the world as curiosity. I was curious, especially about everything that was in me manifesting as thought, intuition, feeling and belief. I was just seeing and being in everything, and it was good. Sometimes thoughts or mind activity would arise and sometimes the appearance was dominant in a way that pulled my attention into it in a compromising way. It was painful, it was suffering, but it had to happen for full embodiment to manifest. I could see that the pull that came from the patterns was not ego, rather it was memory. I could see that standing in liberated knowing was the end of the ego, but not the end of its effects.

There were days of flatness when not much was happening but the seeing was permanent. A new integrity was awakened within that could be reflected without. The constant state of knowing – awareness prior to identified form – was itself okay. Knowing this, and seeing this, it was about standing as formless consciousness as patterns pulled from their attraction to a compromised identification, but the pull to identification is not identification itself. I remained open. The formlessness remained in formless orientation rather than compromising to a form identity.

Maintaining formless integrity is maintaining honesty. I began to experience memories on all dimensions as raw, without identification. Images, thoughts, feeling, physical emotion, all served to feed off consciousness into the very essence of being. By maintaining honesty of awareness I felt the suchness of past ways of being – the suchness being the direct experience of appearance without there being an *I*, formless integrity. The *I* continued to haunt and play out like old movies, short clips of learned old behaviours and beliefs, from coarse to very subtle. Awareness remained in its knowing.

Knowing curiousness would go into everything that would arise, merging because of the formless nature of such free consciousness. In merging I was feeling everything without defence or protection, for any form of protection would be a self-centred orientation that would compromise one's formless identity. Becoming anything for want or need compromises the true knower as formless with the ability to relate from no-thing, or source. It is only as a relating from or to source that changes to the outer reflections of distorted self can happen, maintaining relatedness from source itself. I found this process fascinating, I was doing nothing apart from being totally open to the seeing of everything, and via the seeing came a streaming of essence, realised consciousness, that would dissipate illusion. This living process that I was seeing unfold was pulling me further in. I began to live only for that.

NOTHING KNOWS NOTHING

The outer structure and routine of my life was simple. Functioning was merely a condition that reflected the world's condition. Earning money, roof over the head, security. It all could happen. I was living for truth, letting go of all need for self-preservation. My job could have come to a sudden end and I wouldn't have cared. The world of appearance was simply happening, but what was aware and experiencing that was not here, was not of the world. The world I could see was of *That which Is*, absolute consciousness, oneness. I spent much time alone, walking in Burnham Beeches, merging with the trees, some of the time just staying in my room with the curtains closed.

The outer world of appearance had lost all meaning now. Not just in its definition of what one is but, also, in a way of being. I found that the only way of being was in remaining in my knowing of being. The true movement was not in the world, however much the ego had once deluded itself. The true movement was the attention of awareness maintaining its relation with reality itself, a merging that was a reality orientation. Form could only reflect that. In all forms, there was only *That which Is* experienced as is. Beneath the whole of apparent reality is this emptiness, an undifferentiated consciousness that is the direct experiencer of all things.

I continued to watch people in social and professional settings. I began to see the play of emptiness within people. Wherever there was a person's focus, there was their realised or unrealised emptiness of awareness. To be realised was to know that all outer forms of expression are linked to this empty experiencer, and to know that the experience itself is empty. A nothing that knows nothing within the world of things. Things being the formless manifestation, formless appearing as form, the formless experiencer of form.

I could see how the focus of attention can assume a thought. I began to see the majesty of consciousness, and the wonder of its ability to merge with anything, and in its merging, the direct experience of everything. It was then easy to see that, first, consciousness becomes lost in its learning to merge, so it becomes the same as what it merges with. This distorted merging of consciousness we call identification. This arrested development of awareness can remain in the self at whatever stage, and remain regressed as a person. It is, then, identified as a person, that consciousness continues to relate via the main agent, the mind.

My world became such a mystery. I was more established in my knowing as the reality principle. Holding onto anything didn't matter anymore – even the thought seemed absurd. My knowing consciousness couldn't differentiate between the inner and outer worlds of experience. There was simply a direct experience from prior form. All things were now becoming in line with, or in relation to, knowing. Knowing was not divided by inner and outer experience, it simply was undifferentiated experience itself.

Now that there was a standing in knowing, there was a new seeing of things as they were. It was in the seeing that I had the revelation that it was also the doing. In relation to *That which Is*, the attention of it is also the movement of it. The yin and the yang, male and female, positive and negative. Now there was the recognition, and the relating from. This led to a completely new understanding, and experience of human process.

In knowing no-thing, one is no longer identified as the person; one simply experiences the personal reflections of identity as a movement that arises out of the emptiness. Without the identification, there is just the pattern, the memory of *me* – a personal reflection that now reflects the unity of being, and the suchness of all things, even the *me*. The *me* itself became a personal aspect of the formless expression. The personal sense was not a *me* – rather, it was a quality of consciousness, not an identification.

Using anything in the capacity of self rather than just knowing oneself seemed untrue, or dishonest. Identifying where a person's attention was and to have them know what they were doing with it seemed more appropriate than to engage in a story. Stories of self only go as far as the perceptual self can go. To know it, was to fall through it. It is as consciousness that one falls through the eye of the needle, it is the self that is the eye of the needle.

The world now was so abstract; there just *was* and everything was appearing from it. The attention of consciousness was in relation to the mystery that is called *That*. No words can describe but, as naked awareness, we can know via the surrendered non-identified state.

EMPTINESS MOVES

The world had lost all meaning. Meaning was purely within the realisation of awareness. I moved unseen through appearance, external and internal, via *That* which is neither internal nor external, not form but a movement direct from the field of reality. Knowing and seeing, non-identifying, and being.

I was inspired again, within and without the world. I was honest in who I was, and honest in being that formless identity. More and more the rabbit hole was going deeper. I could not take my eyes away from what I was seeing in other people around me and in myself. Seeing everything, and experiencing everything, proved more and more that there was nothing beneath it all, no *me*, or *I*. Subjective experience was a reflection of an absolute awareness playing out in form. In all form was the one reality.

My feelings still arose, I still felt Hannah as something I longed for. I could see my attachments, and memories of learned holdings of idealised love. This all arose now out of the one. Experiencing this loss of love was to experience my learned resistance to an absolute love. I stood in my knowing that was not in need or want, seeing the need and want of a dear memory arise out of it. It was then that I felt the true connection I had with her. Fear had subsided, the contraction had come undone. There was no one any more, only a connection via a formless streaming of attention that could wait in an eternal place. Connections remain always.

Seeing my undoing was different now. It was not purely seen from an awareness that had merged totally as truth. Awareness was now going anywhere where there was a pull from inner and outer, always reflecting the true ground of being, without identifying with form, thus maintaining a formless integrity. Instead of identifying, I began to merge, or absorb.

Having consented to this process, I feared nothing; no financial insecurity nor anything else. Work continued to be nothing more than a structure that allowed me financial solvency. I lived to simply see. Within the daily structure I remained present, a presence in relation to being. A state prior to form. I found that, by being present, concentrating on the work at hand, other people around me would be too caught up in their own worlds to give attention to me.

MERGING

I could now see that absorption or merging awareness was totally different to identification. I knew from the beginning of realisation that identified consciousness is itself the illusion of a separate self. I could now see that merging is the absolute opposite of identification. Instead of becoming fixed to form as meaning, form reflects the true meaning given by realisation of pure consciousness.

The merging consciousness gives way to the direct experience of form without losing sight of the ultimate oneness of reality.

There was a new freedom. I was merging with people I met, or places, even a woodland walk, and dogs. It was subtle merging in the everyday practical reality, to deep merging in gatherings or one-to-one meetings. I loved the way my knowing just knew what was happening without thinking. The merging quality of consciousness was in itself a joy.

It had been nearly two years since I'd led any sort of normal life — although my life has never been typical in any way. My introspection had come undone. I started coming back into the world. I loved being in the world again because I could *be*. I love cafés. Since my earliest days in recovery, I loved sitting in cafés, watching people, and being with friends. A lot of my recovery was done in this way and so I had an affinity for it. I began sitting in a café in Soho — one that had a cellar where I could write. On a Sunday morning, initially on my own, and then with one or two friends, and then as word got out about my awakening we were joined by others who'd been invited along to 'be with Steve'.

I loved Soho. I love London. I would sit for an hour anywhere in a café, and then just walk around the central city. In London there is so much movement and energy, vibrancy. But within all of the perceptual was the constant knowing of emptiness. I loved being alone and anonymous, connected.

Consciousness maintaining formless recognition, or integrity, was everywhere. I began seeing what I had really needed to see all along, the relation that form has to emptiness, the effects of emptiness upon form. I could now see this living process – the very movement of realisation. The question had been answered. Truth was no longer just a realisation – it was a relation, relation to being.

Remaining true to knowing was consistent, even if the outer patterned self at times could not reflect that. The self would pattern in confusion, and I would come to know my confusion… and just wait. Knowing is a realisation of itself without confusion or any perceptual arising. Confusion is only blinding when, like anything else, there is an identification rather than a merging. Knowing was now established.

The suchness of all things is the experience of all things. A merging of consciousness that relates from the one experiences the one in everything. This relating is spontaneous and happens without any conceptual definition that would construct an I, a me or a mine. There simply just *is*, everything arising. One as pure awareness is spontaneously experiencing as formless and not as form.

The experience of a thought, the suchness of

it, is memory. The memory is usually contracted within one of the emotional centres (or chakras) in the body. When the emotional centre is triggered or touched, it will react as thought. Thought and feeling come from the same place of contracted holding of remembered experience. In merging with thinking, it loses the force of its own identifying projection and, instead, it comes in on itself, returning to the emotional, contracted centre of the body. In doing the same, merging with the emotional patterning, the projective, identifying force of that emotional programme comes in on itself. Going beyond that as consciousness, one then comes into alignment with bodily presence. One returns to being, having had the contraction become activated to the merging power of one's formless integrity. Now, where there was a tight contraction, there is a coming into bodily presence, relating from a naked awareness aware of the deepest existence of formless, unmanifest reality, even in the body. Form imitates consciousness as consciousness itself becomes the formless experience that form itself as a condition reflects.

LOVE OF TRUTH

This interplay of naked awareness merging, and absorbing all experience without losing its knowing of origin, was the love of truth. In coming back into the self, it had to be done this way, without anyone doing anything. The love of truth was no longer purely a recognition, but rather, it was now a complete and utter surrendered state, maintaining recognition of absolute, but also of the formless merging power that consciousness is. Consciousness then becomes a way of being.

For two years I had to sit within all that was arising: a meditation on my own reaction to life. In seeing the reaction I was experiencing truly. For the first time that was aligned with the true action of seeing, and its creative force of being, a being that was relating via recognition, an awareness that I'd come to know, as knowing itself.

I began to see the reaction in other people. I could see now the layer of the egoist identity entity. A contracted memory of experience that had been identified with and crowned as 'me'. Awareness that is not realised knows that something is wrong, but in its own defence it continues to use thought, will, and intuition to create something that thinks and feels better. The 'I' becoming more subtle, and more refined. The only way out of such bondage of self, or self-obsession, was to become no-thing as awareness, and to relate from a knowing that in the beginning simply has no understanding. Understanding only comes with the realisation of absolute. With that comes revelation, an understanding that reflects this recognition. In this shift of consciousness, the true understanding falls deeper than the mind's reflection, so that one's formless knowing, and awareness, becomes that understanding itself without thought to guide.

Thoughts have power. There were times, especially when my relationship with Hannah ended, that thoughts would arise like a pack of dogs. The suchness of this experience let them into me, deeper than the defence that had been available to me in previous relationships. I now relating from the origin that allowed for seeing.

There was a growing natural curiosity around the direct experience of thought and feeling perception, but there was never a crossover into mindbased arrogance of understanding. The experience is always new, always curious. When attention is clean it is the very spearhead of creation. Where you are pure attention, you are changing, not because of want, but because of a true will, and movement that comes from *That* which just *Is*. Life continues but with greater meaning than an ordinary life comes to know.

This meaning in modern terms is called *intimacy*. The biggest fear within the dysfunctional realms of attachment is fear of intimacy. It is a fear of who we are, it is a fear of reality. Instead, as consciousness, we identify with an image we create in order to avoid the truth – a truth that will undo what has been created. This fear when challenged by reality will create a psychic projective defence.

So much was happening now compared to before but it was good, it was painful, it was happening. London on Sundays was beautiful. A beautiful place to move around and experience. A good place also for the negative aspects of patterning to arise. I saw that I was impatient with people in crowds and my reaction could be quicker than my engaged knowing. It surprised me just how much dis-ease was still in me.

The more the patterns arose, the more I experienced without agenda. The memories and patterns are there. There is no idealised way of separating what you want to experience and what you do not. Everything is under review when it comes to knowing. As knowing I was free and undefined, but yet accountable. Regarding the patterning, it had come from me and, now, it must return.

CONTINUAL KNOWING

My life continued now as knowing. The recognition of truth had come into the love of truth. Two years had passed. The self continued its bodily and mental processes of undoing but that undoing was becoming much less. Knowing was becoming more embodied, bodily presence. Knowing within the body was an experience of the body maintaining the formless reality principle of consciousness.

Everything arises out of not-here without separation. Nothing exists outside of consciousness for there is no outside of consciousness. Consciousness itself was *That* which arose out of the unmanifest, and in that merging, knowing again, there is no separation.

The realised awareness is no-thing experiencing the appearance of things. Within our knowing is the choiceless choice of remaining true and honest, an honesty that is of itself and not conceptualised in any way. It does not matter what arises, all is to be seen, and moved through, so that the bodily presence becomes restored to *That* which is experiencing, no separation.

The movement of knowing is a direct reflection of the oneness and unity of all things. Movement is not of the mind but of the realised consciousness that arises out of the absolute. This true movement undoes any outer pattern of non-recognition, or separation. The way of being then becomes reflected within the appearance of outer movement, a reflection of the true movement of *as is*. There is no longer a division that separates, division serves only to reflect.

Knowing itself, as awareness, is an emptiness that reflects the reality that lies beneath all form. This awareness is a division in itself, but a knowing reflecting division where consciousness has come to see itself, and express itself. Knowing was bigger than form now. Everything seemed to arise easily out of the self that arose out of consciousness that arose out of being.

I had grown in the two years by becoming nothing more than a knowing that remained surrendered, and seeing. Life was no longer about the distinction between mind and absolute reality. I was now a knowing of *I Am* that remained despite form's appearance, and it was ok. Between the absolute knowledge and worldly knowledge is that which is known simply as a liberated awareness. An awareness that knows reality and is able to merge with form while remaining formless.

Maintaining reality via a formless awareness leads to the purpose of one's knowing which is to live simply for truth. It's everywhere, you can't miss it; it's the one unified reality that is meaning itself. Relating from source as an awareness of it, there was also seeing it in everyone else, and all things.

There is no more searching, just being. Things are arising in accordance with the laws and principles of the relative dimension of form, but as formlessness there is the direct experience where nothing is needed to be done as the 'doing' is the grace of seeing. This is the purpose of love, to love of itself for itself without anything existing outside of itself. There is no separation.

DIALOGUES

Consciousness Is
the Only Real Experiencer

QUESTIONER: A few weeks ago I had an awakening which then went away again. I'm left with the longing for the depth of being, for the peace and silence of home. I can drop thoughts but, instead of then resting as awareness and feeling that no-thing is my true nature, I'm just left with my attention resting in form.

STEVE: There's the appearance of things, of form, and the recognition you're not this, but without the depth of relating from no-thing.

When a person awakens in the beginning that brings the end of many attachments – a lot of identifications fall away. There's a huge sense of liberation, a real formless sense of awareness amongst everything that's happening, but the condition of life continues, it starts to build up around you again. So instead of relating to it from the liberated sense, you get caught up in it, pulled back into it – you've not yet learned how to negotiate form, you've not learned how to *be* in form, and to allow form to reflect the true experience of no-thing, for these two to come together as one. In other words there's no integration as yet.

So where there's no integration you've been walled up again, your formlessness has been walled back up. All is well, though. This condition arises as a natural extension to consciousness because everything exists in consciousness, there's nothing outside of consciousness. It's just that it no longer feels acceptable after having tasted of your true nature.

So you're seeing clearly, intellectually, but you're not relating from the true depth of *home*. You're no longer identifying with form in the same way, but you're thinking, *Where's the depth?* So in one sense you're awakened to the nature of reality, but you're not *home*.

When I first awoke from identified existence there was relating from absolute consciousness, a non-located consciousness that was in everything. At first there was absolutely no separation, but the conditions of life continued to arise and I began to experience division again within this seeing from oneness. I didn't know how the division reflected oneness. I was seeing, but I wasn't understanding how that moves, or how that relates from Home, how form arises in relation to Home, or consciousness that is realised. These were questions I had to ask myself. Over a period of two years I had to look at everything again.

The best way is to let everything in form be experienced. Don't let it *be* the experience. Allow yourself to be the experiencer – which of course is formless consciousness. If you become the experiencer then form will live in relation to you. As the experiencer you are that awakened consciousness, you are that pure awareness, and there's no need to stop thoughts. Let it all happen but know that it's formless awareness or formless consciousness that is the experiencer. Although arising in and as consciousness all that appears – including thoughts – could be said to be unconscious, because all arising conditions or modifications of consciousness are reflections, nothing but form, memories, shapes, patterns.

So form is just mechanically happening?

It is. But prior to that is the awakened state of non-personal consciousness, formless awareness. Consciousness in its knowing of itself relates from *That which Is*. So that's *home* when you relate from *That which Is*. Someone who relates from *home* can truly speak about it, they can knowingly say everything is one. The person who has had an awakening but has then re-identified with form can't speak from *That*.

So whatever's happening is happening, but if the position as formless awareness, as consciousness, is maintained, you then stop feeding form in a way that is perpetuating the patterns. The only thing that can modify this is the experiencer. Who is the experiencer? Formless consciousness. Maintain formless integrity, relating from *That which Is*, from just being, and allow your attention to be one with everything that's happening. The mind, and all else that's arising out of *That* – all happening – is in that field of consciousness. Allow consciousness to be the experiencer and it all becomes one.

How not to get lost in the mind as it arises, and the forms? How to remain as the experiencer?

There'll be patterns of that, there'll be the sensation of getting lost, there'll be sensations of being confused – that happens within the defence mechanisms and patterns that you've built up over your life. But you know knowing, you know you're consciousness. This is where they say it's too simple. Right now you're seeing from emptiness, from no-thing. You are thinking, you are listening, you are forming your opinion, you're holding everything I say within your already built schema of knowledge, but really, what is experiencing that is no-thing. There is no one, no individual that is the experiencer in truth. Consciousness is the only real experiencer.

So that no-thing is a knowing. That knowing knows, in a way, that it can know no-thing and relate from no-thing; it can be just purely present and formless without identifying with anything. But we know that there is a condition of consciousness that arises – the room, your thoughts, someone else walking into the room – we all have a reaction to that, we all experience that, but the awareness that has learned to move within that without identification relates from purely just awareness, from integrity of formlessness within form. So it's ok to have emotions, feelings and sensations, but who is it happening to? To no one. There is no one. All is consciousness.

Then, what happens is, your attention becomes a pure streaming of consciousness, or essence. And that essence, if it's delivered via a pure realised consciousness, begins to dissipate patterns that are in resistance, or are contracted. So the only thing that can actually 'heal' you is openness. It's a matter of learning, not to see things for the sake of seeing things and saying 'I'm formless', rather it's knowing you're *home*, that *home* is already here prior to this. And your very attention maintaining that reality becomes a modifier of all form. Contractions are loosened, undone. Nothing is out of consciousness, everything is in relation to consciousness, everything is arising in relation to it. So if you're relating from *home* then seeking, and all thoughts of seeking, will simply fall away. They will not take your attention. Your attention, as it goes in there, will dissipate them. If you maintain awareness you'll find that actually begins to modify all form.

So how do I maintain that awareness, how does one stay as the awareness? Just by knowing that everything arising is merely a modification of consciousness?

It's by just simply being aware. Awareness is its own reward, without using anything to define it or understand it. You see, in our talking now, there is an awareness that is aware of this. It's knowing what's being said. We're talking; there is the 'we' which is the condition (manifestation) of consciousness arising out of consciousness, but what's really communicating is no-thing. You and I are prior to this, looking at each other, seeing from a totally different perspective – an intelligent perspective. The modifications of consciousness can live in alignment to that, live in relation to that, but if we're in a state of un-realisation then we get caught up in the story, in the drama.

So having had an awakening there can be the going back into the drama, and getting caught up again?

You have to. There's no other way, unless you've lived the life of a Zen monk and are prepared. But in the west we're not prepared. Most people aren't prepared. We kind of fall into it by accident! You wake up, and suddenly you're a liberated consciousness within a body/mind that is a machine built for separation. What do you do? You can't just go around saying 'That's not me, that's not real'. That's not *home*. That's not relating from *home*. In fact there's a lot of that going on at the moment, because it's easy, it's the easy deal.

What, you mean negating?

Negating and keeping running back to the absolutist — for instance, *Consciousness is emptiness, it's non-identified,* and so forth. But that in itself doesn't teach you how to live as truth in relation to all that's arising.

So you're saying rather than negating it's a matter of simply remaining as no-thing and flowing into whatever arises?
Rather than flowing into, what it feels like is that you're being pulled into, because every form, every

modification of consciousness has a pull, like a magnet – it feeds off the essence. You are the essence. You are the portal for essence. Your attention is the administrator of essence. When I look at you, you can feel my attention – it's an energy.

So can that attention, that energy, facilitate awakening?

Yes, it can have a profound effect on an individual, allowing them to experience something other than mind/body, but whether they become realised in that or not is the question. Whether they're able to resonate in a way where the resonance within them is something they can relate from that is not body/mind, that is prior to body/mind.

So what is that down to? Is that what we would call grace?

It's surrender. It's the letting go of everything.

So it's the acceptance, the allowing of all that's arising...

Totally.

... while just being present as formless awareness?

Yes.

*So to be with someone like yourself who lives con-
sciously from and as no-thing – does that have a kind
of quickening effect?*

When you're with someone who is relating from
prior being, from no-thing, there's the outer play
of words in the form of a conversation, but the real
connection is prior to that. There's a stream of attention that can touch you. It's a streaming that isn't
thought or feeling. It's a stream of consciousness
that is pure attention, that is fully awake to itself as
home, that seeks itself in all things and touches you.

Everyone is doing this, except that with a fully
awakened person it's pure, it's coming in a pure
form, it's not attached to anything, not coming via
ego, so it's touching that in you which is prior to
form. But if someone is not fully awakened and
they're projecting an identification, then you'll still
feel that person's energy but it comes into thought
form, or feeling form, and it's manipulative and it
has an agenda. It's not open and it's not healing in
that sense. It's divisive. It doesn't show you who
you are. It'll help you, maybe hurt you, but it won't
show you truth.

Whereas a person who is fully realised, their
attention is something that can actually open up

things for you. It invites you into *That*. It's nothing to do with thought or feeling. It's about prior presence, about relating from that. That is the surrendered state of consciousness, and in that surrendered state of consciousness one is living prior to form, relating from the non-personal consciousness, from the oneness out of which everything arises. Then you realise you've never been born, never died, and that all is appearing within consciousness.

Partial Realisation

It seems that there are many speakers or teachers relating from a certain level of awakening which is somehow not fully expressing the real deal. There's no real juice in their expression – they seem to be in some sort of halfway house.

Yes, it's just a mind opening – awakened mind – but without the cost of their heart. There's no compassion. Compassion is a direct seeing, a relating from true nature. With a mental opening, there's the defending of an idea, which is an awareness, but it's a born awareness. It knows its orientation isn't of thinking, but it's not as yet surrendered. They're not relating from *home*, from *It*. Their attention is not a flow that is primarily arising out of *That* which cannot be understood. If they were really *home*, relating from true nature, then they would know that the true way of seeing is a compassion and a true action which has no need of defending that there is no one, no individuality in a mental sense. The motivation for that defending comes from the fact that their awakening is dependent purely on a mental opening.

It's been seen that there is no one but it's been seen by an awareness that is still living in relation to their revelation – a living concept which then re-embodies as a mental concept which knows that the mental is not the primary reality.

So when the opening occurs where one sees that they're not their thinking, there is just a clean awareness, there is just a presence of mind. It's very profound, profound on a mental level, but if it just stays there then that becomes the reality principle. There is awareness that the mind is just happening, and then from that observing point you can see that everything else is just happening.

But to die to self is to allow the heart contraction to open, where you go beyond the emotional nature of who you are, which is much much deeper than the nature of mind. The mental condition of humanity is just a ripple compared to the deep undercurrent of emotional identity – the emotional attachment you have with family, friends and others. It is that that you must die to.

So there is the reality principle that yes, you're not mind, but to really die to the illusory is to then allow the deeper contraction to open with consciousness still maintaining its knowing within that. Then consciousness really falls into itself, and totally then relates from itself. In the mental opening, consciousness is not relating directly from itself, it's still in transition, still dying to Self, but it gets stuck in an understanding.

So is it then that the emotional attachments are like a protective covering around the heart?

Yes, emotion is acquired heart meaning. The heart is the deepest capacity for consciousness, how you feel about things. Emotional attachment is the deepest attachment that we have, and it's here (*points to heart*) not up here (*points to head*).

Surrendering to the mind is still quite a big deal, going beyond thinking, but to die to everything and to relate from the absolute is very different.

My Life Has No Meaning
but I Act as if It Does

Can you say something about how you see? What you see, as it would differ from how we're seeing it, or I'm seeing it, if that makes sense?

Where I see from is present, alive, it exists in the moment. Fifteen years ago a shift of consciousness took place, an opening in my life where I could see from, a place of being, a place of no-thing.

Sudden?

Very sudden, yes. Sudden in that it happened in one evening, and it happened in a way where I could see without any distortion coming from my mind or how I'd always perceived things in the past. All fell away, and I could see from true nature, which is what I've come to know as being, as the unmanifest, as stillness, as silence, as Home. I see from a place where there's nothing attached to anything – it just is.

I hadn't been looking for this because I wasn't

a seeker. I had no background in spiritual life, in any kind of spiritual seeking – I didn't know this existed! All I sought was a little bit of honesty in my life. I wanted to go beyond the thoughts and feelings that were getting in the way of my life. My life felt dishonest, kind of crooked, and I knew I didn't see things the way they were. But I had no idea that if I was to let go of what I'd invested in as a reality, an outer reality, beyond that was the no-thing out of which everything arises.

When I came into being, it happened by doing nothing. It happened by self-acceptance. I accepted exactly who I was, who I thought I was, and it wasn't some heroic picture. Instead it was quite sad. I came to accept that my way wasn't the best way, and I didn't know who I was, and that my thinking wasn't right, and my feelings were all over the place. I was struggling and I gave all that back to life as it was.

I could no longer invest in what I'd become. I wasn't trying to justify or search or anything. I just knew what I'd become. I just knew what I thought and what I felt wasn't me. So it wasn't trying to understand it that brought revelation. It was in fact just accepting, really accepting what I'd become, with an ok-ness. Self-acceptance not self-resistance. Not: *What if I do this*, or *If I read that*, or *If I just understood.*

It was a stopping. When I wasn't sure of what was going to happen, I was scared. There was fear because it happened all in one go – there was great fear. But when I let go there was a stillness. Stillness descended in a way that I'd never known stillness. There was no more investing in the meaning that the egoic consciousness needs to survive. Instead there was a stillness, and the mind opened. And the opening of the mind is more profound than any thought that can be born of the mind.

The mind that doesn't know true nature likes a very tight package, likes great understandings. But as soon as there is a deep acceptance, there is a stillness and there is an opening in the mind. For the first time in my life I became aware of silence and stillness in my head, where nothing passed through. No thought. Nothing.

I became aware of this, and as I became aware of it, there was a kind of dropping. I found myself going down, from my head, and at that point the ego wanted to get in there and say: *Whoa! You know, this is scary!* It was going beyond what I knew but, as awareness I consented.

As I dropped further, I felt a very sharp pain in my chest, and there was a thought in my head, just this one thought: *This is what you've been running from all your life – pain, just pain.* I was in my head all my life, and now I was entering into my heart, above which was a layer of pain. I said *ok*, and that's when the ego died. Egoic consciousness totally just fell away and there was an opening.

The mind came away, and where there was no attachment, there was no resistance, it just opened. There was this expansion in my heart, and I remember it was like a void. It just sucked me right in. It just opened and I vanished – everything personal, everything that meant anything in identity that served in this world vanished.

This opening, it just opened and opened and opened. I vanished and there was just openness, this amazing openness, this amazing presence – being. And I could see from a non-personal place. I'd gone beyond the ego – or should I say, the ego just fell away.

The following day when I was walking around, it was like: *I'm free!* I felt no restriction. There was no Steve, whereas before there used to be this self-conscious, self-obsessed guy who was just terrified of the world, and suddenly I wasn't there anymore.

It's a different way of seeing things, seeing things directly rather than through the filter of contractions and knots that is ego. The very next day I started to see people, the world, in a totally different way, and I was unprepared for it. When I spoke to people, I wanted to tell them about what had happened, about my new-found honesty – for that's what I thought it was in the beginning, just pure honesty. I could see without judgment, without stain.

You still felt separate from people?

No. Where I could see from, the unmanifest, I could see that the same being was in them, but sleeping. This is how I experienced it. I could see that people were primarily relating from their minds, which defines how they know things within the relative world. But what they couldn't do was see from the unmanifest, the world of intimacy and being, the world of love and oneness.

Ah! I see, oh my God I see, my mind is gone – stillness, being, infinity. Where I was seeing from was very impersonal, it was as if life itself was seeing through me. And yet, in that, I found myself as an expression of being. So I was one from an absolute level and also on a personal level – which of course are one and the same. I was nothing more than an expression, coming into form.

So when I started talking to people, I found straightaway that what I got was a projection, not intimacy. Projection is a different energy – mind energy, which is different to being energy. Their mind projection was here, talking, and they would be looking at with 'perceptual eyes' not 'seeing eyes'. 'Seeing eyes' are just openness. I could see directly with no blocks or contractions.

I could see people with a look in their eyes like an agenda – the mind's agenda: *What are you saying? What do you mean? I don't understand that! I don't know where you're coming from.* I wasn't prepared for this – these identities projecting all around me.

So then I began to think that this was bigger than I'd thought. There was no way I could doubt what had happened to me. When you fall into truth, you know it's truth – although I didn't have the language to describe it then. The mind lies down when it is permeated and undone by truth. But then you rediscover your mind – there's a kind of a resurrection where in rediscovering your mind it becomes useful as something that no longer dominates you. It is a function.

I was talking to people whose minds were dominating them, projecting meaning, and the meaning didn't come from being, from the eternal, from truth. In their eyes I could see life, but it was diminished, it was pushed down, it was kind of sleeping, behind the projection. That's how, on awakening, I first started to see people.

It's still kind of the same, except that now, several years later, I am able to see and facilitate openings in people. Suddenly the mind is set aside and there's a connection on a being level.

Did you come across people who were also relating directly from being?

No, none.

Must have been quite lonely?

I was alone yes. I was alone, intimately alone with my aloneness. Interestingly, though, in the year 2000, *The Power Of Now* by Eckhart Tolle was published, and it was the first time I saw how what had happened to me happened to someone else in exactly the same way, as described in the foreword of that book – the coming into consciousness.

It was interesting talking to people when they were reading that book. They were getting caught up in it, but on a mind level. Their minds were doing stuff with it... I didn't see anyone undone, seeing.

I didn't really talk about it after that. A long period of integration followed until a few of years ago when I began to meet with people who were seeking, who were genuinely asking questions and that's when I really started to connect with people.

Getting undone is like an impossible dream really, because I know my life has no meaning as such but I act as if it does have meaning. I can't stop doing it – like a habit.

Yes. That's how it is, that's the nature of the mind that doesn't know its true nature, although it comes from your true nature – this awesome power in you as consciousness. But it's stuck to a story, to a meaning, to form. The beautiful thing is, though, when you begin to see that the meaning you give it isn't truth, it's something you can stop investing in, believing in.

Is Consciousness a Thing, or Is It a Process?

Is consciousness a thing, or is it a process? Is it a process of beingness, or is it in itself something?

When I came into being it was a great revelation to know who I really was. I came to know that in true nature we are no-thing. So you couldn't say true nature or being, or consciousness is a thing, it's no-thing. It's nothing. Things, or forms, are separate, they are manifestations that arise from nothing. Consciousness comes from nothing, from the unmanifest. But then from the unmanifest, it comes into form. As humans we are kind of in-between. We see from the unmanifest, we see from no-thing. That is consciousness. Yet that seeing is filtered through the ego.

But seeing from *That which Is* sees the suchness in everything, sees things as they are. There's a connection of being with things, with form, but without identification. In that there's oneness. I could say that in my awakening I came to know no-thing – but from no-thing comes everything. It's like sound – when you hear the bells, or you hear music, you hear it comes from silence. Everything comes from silence, comes from no-thing, comes from the unmanifest. So the unmanifest is no-thing, yet it's your true nature. It's who you are. You are from nothing, but from it comes everything. The nothingness is in everything, because everything is a manifestation of nothing.

In Zen they say: *Know your face before you were born*. Before you were born there was no body, no mind, no mental faculty. But there you were as consciousness that was, is and shall ever be – the eternal quality. The mind can't understand this, because the mind is merely a manifestation of this.

So, when you come to know your true nature, you exist as no-thing, you exist as being, and in being everything arises. You see a thought come, a feeling, and there's a sense of seeing all that's arising rather than identifying, personalising. In this seeing there's love, an intimacy; it's the bottom line of what everyone is looking for in their seeking within form, whatever the mode of that seeking.

Aware of Awareness

Steve, do I have to have absolutely come to the end of my tether, as you did – a kind of terminal suffering if you like – or can I surrender, or be in any particular way, or do anything else that will act as a catalyst for my own awakening to true nature?

Maintain awareness without identification with form. Although awareness before realisation has a self-expressed basis, it can, however, be aware of itself as awareness.

This form of awareness is acceptance, an acceptance that is purely aware without having to do anything to attempt to alter or modify the conditions of existence.

Most people don't live as surrendered awareness. Instead, the ego seeks to find truth, but the ego projection cannot find truth. That which is prior to ego is truth.

As awareness no longer actively identifying with form there is a falling into a deeper resonance than mind. When you don't identify with mind it begins to weaken as an identity. In its undoing awareness rests more in what is deeper than mind energy. It becomes aware of the underlying knowing that is not of the grosser self-expression, and it is within this knowing that there is the peace and stillness that ego seeks in outer form.

So, maintaining awareness without identification, is this something we can carry on with in our lives without necessarily coming to sit with you, or would you say the regular connecting is an essential part of this? I mean, what about those who live far distant and aren't able to come into the company of someone like yourself who lives from and as true nature?

Managing awareness as aware of itself can be carried out throughout the day. You will experience your life then as a spiritual practice although not in the more traditionally outward sense. Unidentified awareness then begins to become more familiar than form's projection of a distorted identified awareness.

Recourse comes from finer knowing, wherever you are, whoever you're with. It comes into being via your honest attention that no longer has attachment to form for meaning, or the seeking of meaning. To be with one who already relates to life from true nature is an advantage, but this is not about the swapping of concepts. There is a connection at the deepest level which is prior to form. Being with such a one short-circuits identification with form and assists in maintaining formless integrity. It's where knowing meets knowing.

Is that transmission? How does that work?

I'm not fond of that way of expressing it. Rather, simply sitting with someone who relates from true nature, whoever they may be, is the expression of the very essence of what you are. Essence is the foundation of all that arises out of the one. All appears and is sustained by essence. Upon conscious realisation, and realignment, consciousness becomes the very recognition of that essence. In the recognition, one's attention becomes the administrator, streaming that essence.

Your non-recognition of your deeper knowing of truth is the opposite of that streaming of pure attention. Instead, it distorts. Forms then appear as separate from the source, separate in recognition of their origin. Separation of this knowing breeds an individuality seemingly without unity. Without unity, there is no wholeness, without wholeness comes neediness. Neediness in its distortion creates, in its own image of compulsion, a bodily presence of psychic force alone, without the intimacy of profound insight of our true nature.

If your living has become such that you yearn to

come *home,* and yet that psychic force holds strong sway, then it's likely that at some stage you'll find a connection with one who relates directly from and as formless awareness. This is not, after all, a life of totally arbitrary happenings. Regardless of how it may seem, all – including the grossest of outward experience – is totally connected in the love of the one that we all are.

So, you said just now that, in managing attention as being aware of itself, you will experience your life as a spiritual practice. Does that mean then that a major crisis such as you experienced prior to your awakening isn't necessary as such, that we can in fact just become more aware of awareness as a gradual thing? Is it that you're saying that the most important thing is the commitment to honesty, to integrity, to want more than anything else to see and know from/as true nature?

Yes. Honesty of consciousness is an awareness no longer using the projection of egoic need. The need as a projection starts to come in rather than go out. As awareness, we begin to become aware of the deeper meaning of our false self-projection. Need reveals itself as a deep insecurity, as fear.

Instead of awakening in a sudden dramatic way, we are simply, and honestly, going beyond what we know as needy reference, or reference of the false self and, instead, finding the meaning which is deeper than need within our knowing of unified being.

Our unified being is the *I Am. I Am* is the knower of deeper-than-form security. It knows wholeness, a unified state of awareness before the rising of thought or feeling.

A major crisis is not needed, only honesty of conscious awareness. It is seen then that there is no bigger or smaller crisis. Our honesty leads below all projected dishonesty and illusion. We begin to know, prior to all perceptual patterning. Knowing in itself then becomes the commitment without doing anything other than knowing the truth of being as the foundation of reality.

In the connection with me, I'm inviting you to have a direct experience of *That which Is* without the use of mind. The mind can interpret a deeper resonance but it cannot stand in it, or relate. Only as unidentified awareness can there be merging and relating from the absolute.

The Mind Doesn't Awaken

Your words completely confound the mind. It's like consciousness speaking to consciousness without any seeming acknowledgement of the suffering 'I', of the seeker. So words become redundant really. Questions become redundant, because there can only be a question from an apparent suffering 'I' wanting relief.

But then the question will reflect what is unrealised in the seeker. If their suffering and separation is manifest within a question that is seeking, then all I can do is know their suffering, know their unrealisation, but reflect that from realisation. The mind cannot grasp that.

I find when I'm in your company I become uncomfortably aware of my wanting something from you. There's a heightened awareness of little tight bits and grasping bits because you're completely refusing to give any reality to that in me.

Yes. That impulse in you, that grasping impulse, that condition, will never awaken, which makes it more uncomfortable for you. I'm reflecting you without doing anything with that.

Exactly!

It's just not an intellectual debate is it?

No! In the presence of seekers do you feel a grasping energy coming from them?

Yes, the mind is an impulse that actually cuts off the flow, the openness. It's projected rather than related from or touched – there's no merging. The impulsive thought cannot relate from source. It doesn't recognise source, so if you're in a state of openness and relating from knowing and someone is projecting their mind at you, there's nothing you can say, there's nothing you can say to the mind. The mind doesn't awaken. Whatever you say the only thing the mind will want to pick up is some clever dialogue and understanding. So if I was to go into an outer expression, a mental expression in relation to the mind, it would just be a mental activity. It would just go on and on and on. It never gets fed because it never finds, it never comes into relation to truth. This is why talking about it isn't it. The mind is an ever-hungry mouth.

It's Consciousness Itself That Awakens

What you describe seems so simple, and yet it seems so hard to actually find our true nature.

The seeking is happening as a condition arising in consciousness. Consciousness at play, seeking itself. Just accept that, otherwise you're so busy trying to do something with what's arising as a condition of consciousness to notice what the condition is arising *in*.

There's nothing to be done with the conditions, or modifications, of consciousness. The conditioning is an automaticity – patterning. It's not what goes *home* – it can't, it's merely a reflection. It's consciousness itself that awakens to its own true nature – not a pattern, not the mind. Consciousness is prior to the conditions, or modifications, arising within it – form, thinking, feeling. Our true nature is the formless presence that is prior to that.

What to do then?

Nothing! Whatever is arising within consciousness

as its modification will continue to arise. Nothing needs to be done to it. The impulse to come *home* arises in the midst of the conditions of life but is a call from a deeper place, from *That which Is*, from what we are in truth. When we become truly tired of that outward impulse of seeking, the possibility arises of attention turning to itself, becoming aware of its identification with form, realising that truth can't be found in a reflection.

What is aware of the world, of the modifications of consciousness? Where are you really seeing from? To become aware of this, to become aware as awareness, as consciousness, is the turning around. Form continues to arise as a reflection in consciousness but attention is no longer animating form in the same way, as though the truth of existence can be found within it by seeking.

So do I need to wait until I awaken as you did?

No, that's just more seeking. Just stop! Be aware. Be aware that you're aware. Abide as awareness and maintain that disposition. Allow all arising to continue to arise and cease giving it attention and energy. Know that you are already seeing from oneness, as oneness, from and as true nature.

Three Purposes

Why would consciousness want to identify as form? What purpose does it serve?

There is no real purpose to consciousness identifying with form, that is why it comes to be seen as an illusion – an illusion based on thought. Relating from thought is seen as a reaction to form seeming to be separated from its source and appearing as an individual.

The purpose is relative – a movement or play within consciousness, and that purpose is purely realisation; consciousness knowing itself again as such, knowing itself prior to all arising form. It is as empty, unidentified awareness that full realisation happens, because thought is merely a condition of consciousness and cannot realise in the sense that we mean here. However, although there is no separate individual there is the appearance of one, and realised consciousness relates through, but prior to, the seeming individual.

Awareness, as a prior-to-form knowing, merges with the body-mind, and the body-mind in its relative condition reflects the formless and intimate experiencer – which is prior realised consciousness. The body-mind, or self, then reflects oneness, sees as oneness, allowing the formless experiencer to merge with all forms, experiencing as oneness. The purpose of this experiencing is the love of truth being seen and experienced without compromising the beauty of formless experience.

So, then, the first purpose within consciousness is to realise consciousness itself, via formless and unattached awareness dis-identifying with the illusionary identification with form. It is by relating from that truth of formless awareness that all things are truly seen in their actual relation to being. All illusion of separateness is transcended. Following these two realisations it is seen that the purpose of truth is to live for that, recognising that in all things. The individual is then seen as one who realises no-thing, relating from no-thing, living for no-thing, as no-thing, appearing as someone!

A Connection Prior To All Form

Last time I met with you it felt to me like a silent awareness looking through these eyes looking into silent awareness emptiness through your eyes, and when you left I felt like I had no head, I just could not locate myself, I didn't feel solid at all. Anyway, that wore off that evening and the next day. A felt sense of identity crept back and there was sometimes feeling myself as empty awareness and sometimes not.

What is the value of that expansion? There was emptiness, lack of identity, but then it kind of closed in again and didn't last beyond a few hours.

When we first connected there was a merging of consciousness prior to all conditions; there was just awareness upon awareness, awareness in its recognition of awareness – awareness without attachment to the body, or attachment to this location for its meaning.

Then you experienced a connection prior to all form. In our connecting awareness prior to form was able to merge, and in its merging your awareness experienced realised consciousness, without location. That is, prior to form there is no location, and there was then a relating from that for you because you were that, you were formless. Where I related from, what I saw in you, I touched you and you responded. You responded from *That* which I touched in you prior to form's expression, just pure awareness and the relating from pure awareness prior to conditions.

Then when we parted there was still *That* that had been touched, and from *That* that had been touched there was your response as non-located awareness. But as you came away from the merging then you came away from a deeper relating where consciousness is in pure recognition of itself. As you came away from that you entered into the world and the conditions then arose. In our connecting there was no conditioning – the conditioning had fallen away.

But when you come away from that, you walk down the street and the condition of walking will arise out of you, and as pure consciousness, as pure awareness, that will demand your attention. Your attention then enters back into the world; it begins to match the world in its knowing of what this dimension is all about via your conditional identity, and then as you match it you lose yourself. You are unable to go *home* because you don't understand the nature of matching the condition. You identify with the condition, and because you've always done this with the condition, your resistance to the condition has been your identification.

So instead of matching the condition via your knowing and allowing the experiencing of the condition to be formless consciousness/awareness, you go back into the idea of your condition, which is a complete compromise to your true identity at your expense. Simply put – you have not yet mastered the art of awareness.

How does one master the art of awareness?

By being that in everything. No matter what condition arises maintain your formless presence, maintain your formless awareness that relates from non-location. As your attention is brought into whatever form arises, allow for a surrender, which means to allow for pure matching to occur. Allow yourself to be brought into all arising forms, and that matching will simply be your knowing of what it is that is arising in you, accepting that everything that arises out of you is simply what you have learned, that is conditioned.

With a separated idea in conflict with the condition. That is separation. That is what happened to you. You just don't yet know how to accept your condition.

If change is to occur it will come from your attention that is prior to the conditions, rather than from being caught up in the conditions with a separated idea in conflict with the conditions. That is separation. That is what happened to you. You just don't yet know how to accept your condition.

There's a wanting to and a longing to, but the actual experience betrays that, it seems.

The experience will always reflect, never betray you. As an experiencer without an attachment to the mind for its own definition, consciousness merges with everything without any like or dislike. What you are coming to know is your condition, but your condition is not experiencing it: you, consciousness, are the experiencer. By remaining non-attached but matching you allow for a healing into wholeness.

Knowing Nothing

When I look at the stormy skies I kind of feel a time-lessness inside which I love. I just wonder whether that is truth speaking or maybe it's just a drama and I'm caught in it, that it's just the feeling it gives me.

You can never feel reality. It's like the sound of the bell doesn't go back and touch the bell. The sound of the bell goes out. Feelings go out, they rise out of consciousness, they don`t suddenly spring back and grab the experience of timelessness.

But yes, there is of course the eternal timeless-ness within you, and when you see from that place and are looking at the stormy skies there's a connec-tion. The mind needs to weave its narrative within this, though – it personalises it and there's a sense of separation. That's why you're unsure whether it's truth speaking or just a personal feeling.

I understand what you are saying, but I keep jumping back into my constructs. Realising this I'm beginning to stop doing it and things are beginning to fall away, so that I've got to the point where I see more quickly before getting stuck into the constructs.

In seeing directly from the timeless, from no-thing, there can be a suspension of self, and in that suspension of self there's timelessness, a timelessness in you where a portal opens. Then there's no personal, no difference between the skies and the feelings that arise out of consciousness.

I understand that, I've just never been able to step into it before.

Yes. Stepping into it is seeing directly from it, instead of being aware of it via identification. Do you understand? That is the shift in consciousness. So, when there's direct seeing you see the suchness of all things. Then, whether it's a thought, a feeling, an idea or a beautiful sky, it's clear seeing, rather than being aware via mind.

Alienation is when we are *aware* of truth but are still relating from mind and feelings and are aware that it doesn't conform to true consciousness. There's still separation. Step into consciousness, see *from*, and allow everything in, everything.

Yes. I haven't been able to do that before, but that's what's been happening more the last couple of days – seeing it and letting it in; seeing something and not doing old stuff with it, or making a construct out of it, or contending with what I see or running from it. I've never been able to do this before but lately I'm beginning to. Gradually through our contact I'm coming to this point.

You need to see the personal the way you see the sky. That is all. You can't escape into the sky, and you can't escape into the personal. Escaping into the sky and running away from the personal is the same thing. There is great beauty when one sees the personal and lets it in – something dies and is reborn. Something unbends, un-distorts, and then conforms – that is death and rebirth. Death is the undoing, the unbending, letting it in, allowing it in as consciousness sees, and then there is a conforming which unbends to the true nature of who you are as consciousness. In unbending, then, there is the birth of the newness of consciousness.

I don't know if I'll ever properly get there. I think trying to understand has often been a stumbling block for me and that trying to understand gets in the way.

Your understanding is aware of truth but is not of truth and there will come a day when it will simply drop and truth will be revealed.

I feel like I'm going through that at the moment, I feel it started a couple of days ago, I've taken a step that's taking me there.

You're describing your map. That is your mind, that is the mind's way of understanding a process that doesn't exist. You want to understand so you need a map. You're working on your map. You're walking a path that really is a self that knows not its true nature, but it's doing the best it can in searching for it. The searcher doesn't really exist. That's the mind, the pseudo self.

I'm really understanding what you are saying Steve.

There'll come a point where you no longer need to understand. It fails you and you let everything go – you let every little bit of understanding go. Really it's just a stopping

So the seeing comes at the end of the path and it's seen that the path was a construct?

There's never a path. But a point comes where you just see that the body-mind doesn't hold truth and you actually know nothing. Knowing nothing is an expression of true nature which is no-thing. So, knowing nothing is what you are in truth.

*I understand what you said and I know it. I haven't
dropped into no-thing like you but I understand.*

Of course you understand, that's your way,
to seek understanding. Then one goes beyond
understanding.

Realisation Is Seeing, Not Thinking

When we all meet, Steve, it feels to me as if we don't even really need to say anything, to ask any questions.

In meeting, in sitting together there is a oneness. The mind doesn't know what to do with it and so the mind can come to rest. So then there can be a sense of that oneness, a sense of that stillness and being, uncharacterised by anything.

What separates is when conditioned consciousness doesn't know its true source as no-thing. But from no-thing there is a calling to all conditions. From your own true nature there is a call for wholeness, calling back the conditioning that does not know itself.

The resistance to this is the play of existence. Ego resists the call. It doesn't know how to steer itself into being. It feels a deep undercurrent, a deep resonance, a wisdom that falls beneath it. True nature calls, a true calling that comes from stillness. Stillness of seeing that is not born out of experience, but born out of being.

We ask questions because we think that understanding is going to get us somewhere.

Yes, thinking is looking for what it is not, so more thinking and talking won't give you what you really want. What you really want is already the case anyway but goes unrecognised in the flurry of mind activity. When you sit with someone who is truly *home* then, yes, of course there may well be talking but, as you have observed, even the silent presence of such a one is an undermining influence on the conditions of life.

Identified thinking short-circuits the flow of life. Realisation is seeing, not thinking. It's seeing from no-thing, the unmanifest. Seeing from no-thing you see your thinking. Then thinking reflects what you know, not what it thinks. Knowing and thinking become one and thinking is no longer separated, caught within its illusion of time. There's expansion, there's beingness. When knowing is reflected, you reflect intimacy, you relate directly from being. The mind becomes one with being.

Be OK with Everything

Sometimes I'm able to see very clearly that I'm the awareness in which all this is appearing, but the pull into thought and suffering is often too strong for me to stay with it.

Awareness is ok with all of that. Awareness doesn't diminish in any way does it? Does your presence diminish in any way? It's natural that there's aversion to being lost in thought. With the born awareness there's a built-in aversion or attraction to whatever's going on relatively. If there's hopelessness then be ok with it. Be ok even with that narrow focus on aversion. As you know, none of that defines who you are. Who you are is totally ok with all of that.

From a realisation point of view there's a pure attention that can move within that. So it's not relating from understanding and speaking on behalf of your contraction that is breaking down. As the contraction is breaking down there is a sharp focus to try to avert that. It's fine, all of that is fine, but instead you could just be ok with it, which allows you to be the awareness which is prior to all of that. It is your knowing, it is formless attention. Nothing takes or adds to that, nothing.

So the appearance of all of this, and the aversion to it, are one and the same. The breaking down and the wanting it to get better are the same thing. It's two sides of the same coin. It requires your attention. Because it is a condition of consciousness it requires consciousness. If you can, instead of speaking on behalf of and being stuck in the aversion and the attraction, just relate from presence itself, and you'll be able to move in there. The modification will come from that, from just seeing.

Once you have the clear attention then attention can go into the aversion to what you are, which is the abstraction of it, the contraction. That may continue anyway, but you don't have to relate solely from that aversion and be so caught up in it. There is a much subtler awareness prior to that condition which is just really ok with all of that. In relating from prior to the condition, from pure awareness, everything is allowed, but it's also likely that the contraction will dissolve anyway simply by being aligned with your seeing.

With thanks to:

Doreen Mcanuff
David Barker
Steven Winwright
Lynne Barton
Eva Raud Adamson

Books *from*
Non-Duality Press

If you enjoyed this book you might be interested in other titles published by Non-Duality Press.

Conscious.tv is a TV channel which broadcasts on the internet at www.conscious.tv. It also has programmes shown on several satellite and cable channels around the world including the Sky system in the UK where you can watch programmes at 8.30 pm every evening on channel No. 192. The channel aims to stimulate debate, question, enquire, inform, enlighten, encourage and inspire people in the areas of Consciousness, Non-Duality and Science. It also has a section called 'Life Stories' with many fascinating interviews.

There are over 200 interviews to watch including several with communicators on Non-Duality including Richard Bates, Burgs, Billy Doyle, Bob Fergeson, Jeff Foster, Steve Ford, Suzanne Foxton, Gangaji, Greg Goode, Scott Kiloby, Richard Lang, Francis Lucille, Roger Linden, Wayne Liquorman, Jac O'Keefe, Mooji, Catherine Noyce, Tony Parsons, Halina Pytlasinska, Genpo Roshi, Satyananda, Richard Sylvester, Rupert Spira, Florian Schlosser, Mandi Solk, James Swartz, Art Ticknor, Joan Tollifson, and Pamela Wilson. There is also an interview with UG Krishnamurti. Some of these interviewees also have books available from Non-Duality Press.

Do check out the channel as we are interested in your feedback and any ideas you may have for future programmes. Email us at info@conscious.tv with your ideas or if you would like to be on our email newsletter list.

WWW.CONSCIOUS.TV

Lightning Source UK Ltd.
Milton Keynes UK
UKOW03f1502240914

239096UK00004B/407/P